HOW TO DRAW MAMMOTHS
AND OTHER PREHISTORIC ANIMALS

Mark Bergin

PowerKiDS
press

New York

Published in 2012 by The Rosen Publishing Group, Inc.
29 East 21st Street, New York, NY 10010

Editor: Rob Walker
U.S. Editor: Kara Murray

Library of Congress Cataloging-in-Publication Data

Bergin, Mark.
 Mammoths and other prehistoric animals / by Mark Bergin. — 1st ed.
     p. cm. — (How to draw)
 Includes index.
 ISBN 978-1-4488-6462-1 (library binding) — ISBN 978-1-4488-6471-3 (pbk.) —
 ISBN 978-1-4488-6472-0 (6-pack)
 1. Dinosaurs in art—Juvenile literature. 2. Prehistoric animals in art—Juvenile literature. 3.
 Drawing—Technique—Juvenile literature. I. Title.
 NC780.5.B473 2012
 743.6—dc22

2011017646

Manufactured in China

CPSIA Compliance Information: Batch #SW2102PK:
For Further Information contact Rosen Publishing,
New York, New York at 1-800-237-9932

PAPER FROM
SUSTAINABLE
FORESTS

Contents

Making a Start

Learning to draw is about looking and seeing. Keep practicing and get to know your subject. Use a sketchbook to make quick drawings. Start by doodling, and experiment with shapes and patterns. There are many ways to draw. This book shows only some methods. Visit art galleries, look at artists' drawings, see how friends draw, but above all, find your own way.

5

Drawing Materials

Try using different types of drawing paper and materials. Experiment with charcoal, wax crayons, and pastels. All pens, from felt-tips to ballpoints, will make interesting marks. You could also try drawing with pen and ink on wet paper.

Silhouette is a style of drawing that mainly uses solid black shapes.

Hard **pencils** are grayer and soft pencils are blacker. Hard pencils are graded as #4 (the hardest) through #3 and #2½. A #1 pencil is a soft pencil.

Felt—tip

Felt—tips come in a range
of line widths. The wider
pens are good for filling in
large areas of flat tone.

Lines drawn in **ink** cannot be
erased, so keep your ink
drawings sketchy and less rigid.
Don't worry about mistakes as
these lines can be lost in the
drawing as it develops.

Ink

7

Perspective

If you look at any object from different viewpoints, you will see that the part that is closest to you looks larger and the part farthest away from you looks smaller. Drawing in perspective is a way of creating a feeling of depth, or of showing three dimensions on a flat surface.

The vanishing point (V.P.) is the place in a perspective drawing where parallel lines appear to meet. The position of the vanishing point depends on the viewer's eye level. Sometimes a low viewpoint can give your drawing added drama.

V.P.

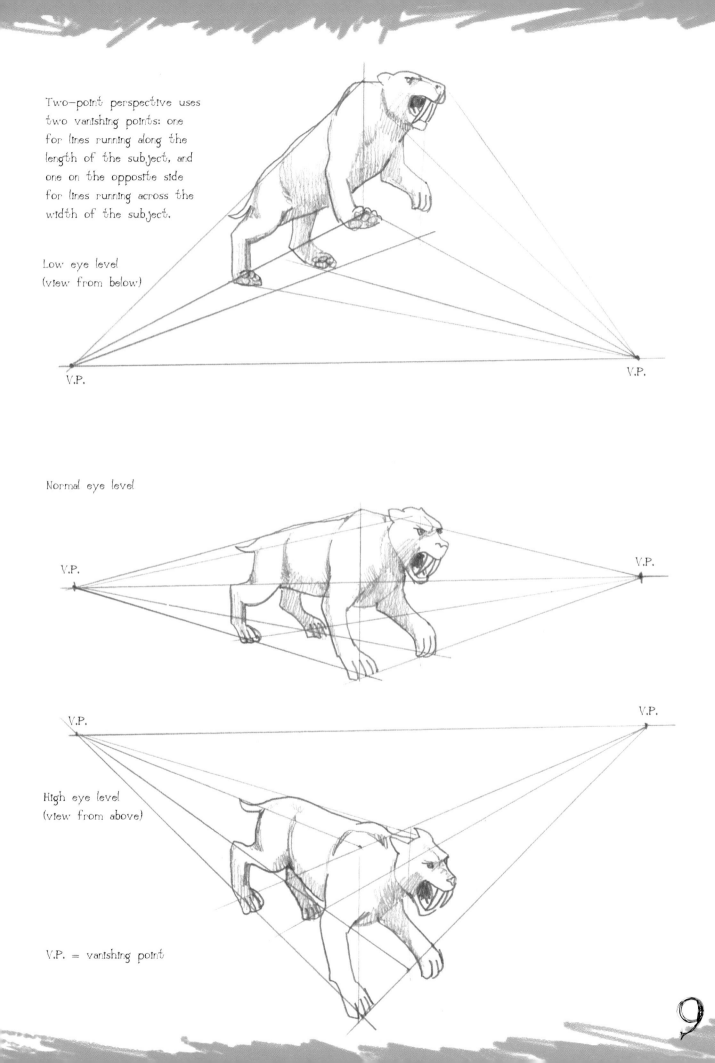

Two-point perspective uses
two vanishing points: one
for lines running along the
length of the subject, and
one on the opposite side
for lines running across the
width of the subject.

Low eye level
(view from below)

V.P.   V.P.

Normal eye level

V.P.   V.P.

V.P.   V.P.

High eye level
(view from above)

V.P. = vanishing point

9

Sketching

You can't always rely on your memory, so you have to look around and find real—life things you want to draw. Using a sketchbook is one of the best ways to build up drawing skills. Learn to observe objects. See how they move, how they are made and how they work. What you draw should be what you have seen. Since the 13th century, artists have used sketchbooks to record their ideas and drawings.

Sketching from toys or models can help you understand the three-dimensional aspects of animals.

Visiting a museum with a prehistoric exhibit is a good place to start your sketches. It will help you understand the form of the animals and their proportions.

Try doing quick sketches as well as more detailed ones. Both will help you improve your drawing skills.

Macrauchenia

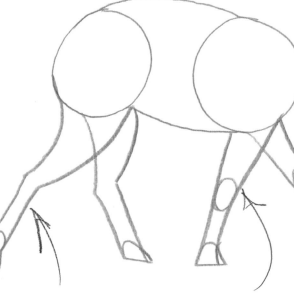

This weird-looking herd creature is found in fossils from South America and lived about 7 million to 20,000 years ago. Charles Darwin found the first fossil of this animal on his voyage aboard the *Beagle*.

Start by drawing two ovals.

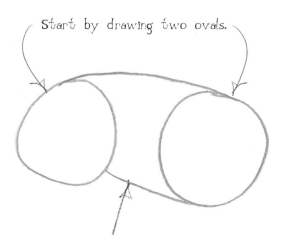

Add two curved lines to connect the ovals.

Add hoof shapes.

Add the back legs. They have curved lines at the top, switching to straight lines for the lower half.

Sketch in the shape of the front legs, adding a circle at the joints.

Key Characteristics

Paying particular attention to the key characteristics can help your drawing work. Specific shapes for the head and hooves or feet can define an animal.

12

Add two curved lines for a neck to connect the head to the body.

Draw an oval for the head.

Position the eye and ears.

Add curved lines for the tail.

Indicate the jawline.

Add the small trunklike nose.

Complete the details of the head.

Add dark tone running up the back of the Macrauchenia to show its markings.

Use the construction lines as a guide to add muscle structure.

Add a mountainous background with trees and grass.

Add darker tone to areas where light would not reach.

Soften some of the lines to show the texture of the fur.

Remove any unwanted construction lines.

13

Andrewsarchus

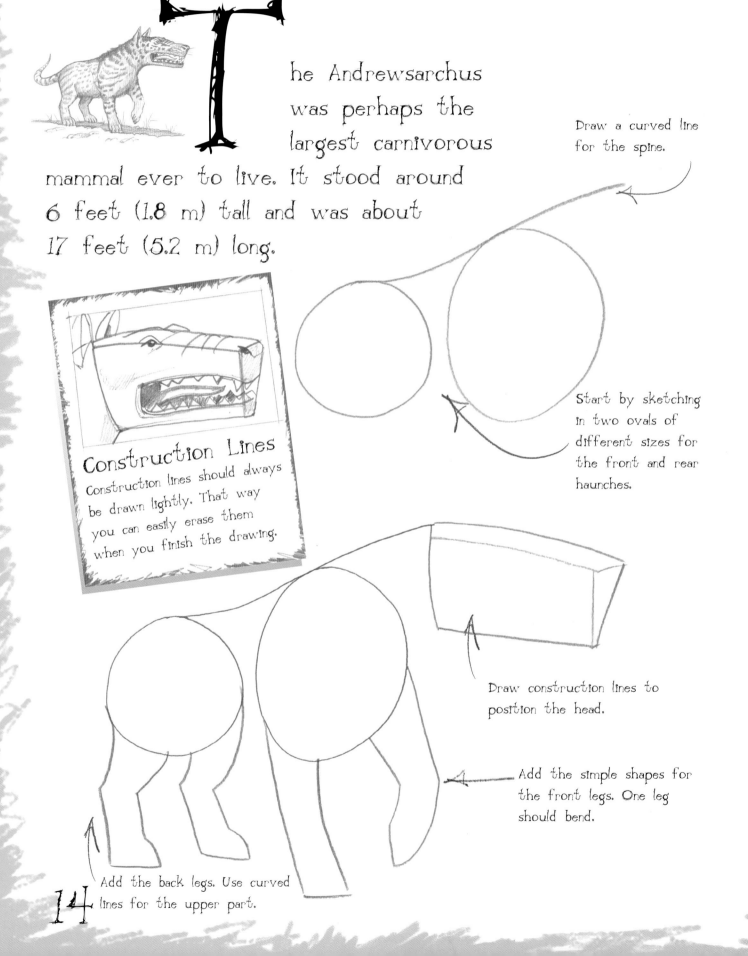

The Andrewsarchus was perhaps the largest carnivorous mammal ever to live. It stood around 6 feet (1.8 m) tall and was about 17 feet (5.2 m) long.

Construction Lines

Construction lines should always be drawn lightly. That way you can easily erase them when you finish the drawing.

Draw a curved line for the spine.

Start by sketching in two ovals of different sizes for the front and rear haunches.

Draw construction lines to position the head.

Add the simple shapes for the front legs. One leg should bend.

Add the back legs. Use curved lines for the upper part.

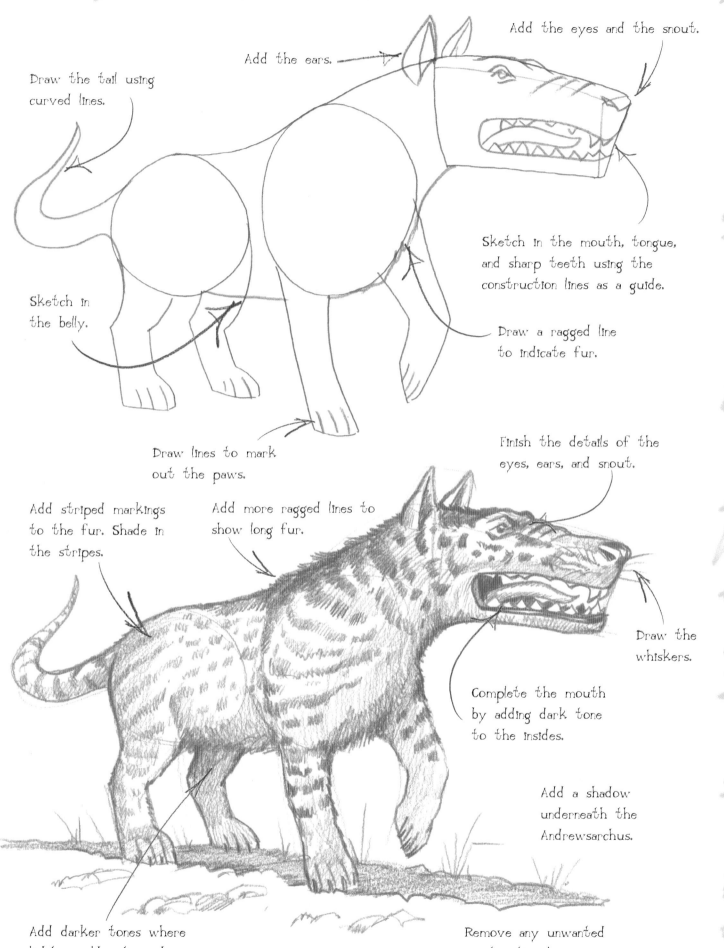

Draw the tail using curved lines.

Add the ears.

Add the eyes and the snout.

Sketch in the mouth, tongue, and sharp teeth using the construction lines as a guide.

Sketch in the belly.

Draw a ragged line to indicate fur.

Draw lines to mark out the paws.

Finish the details of the eyes, ears, and snout.

Add striped markings to the fur. Shade in the stripes.

Add more ragged lines to show long fur.

Draw the whiskers.

Complete the mouth by adding dark tone to the insides.

Add a shadow underneath the Andrewsarchus.

Add darker tones where light would not reach.

Remove any unwanted construction lines.

15

Basilosaurus

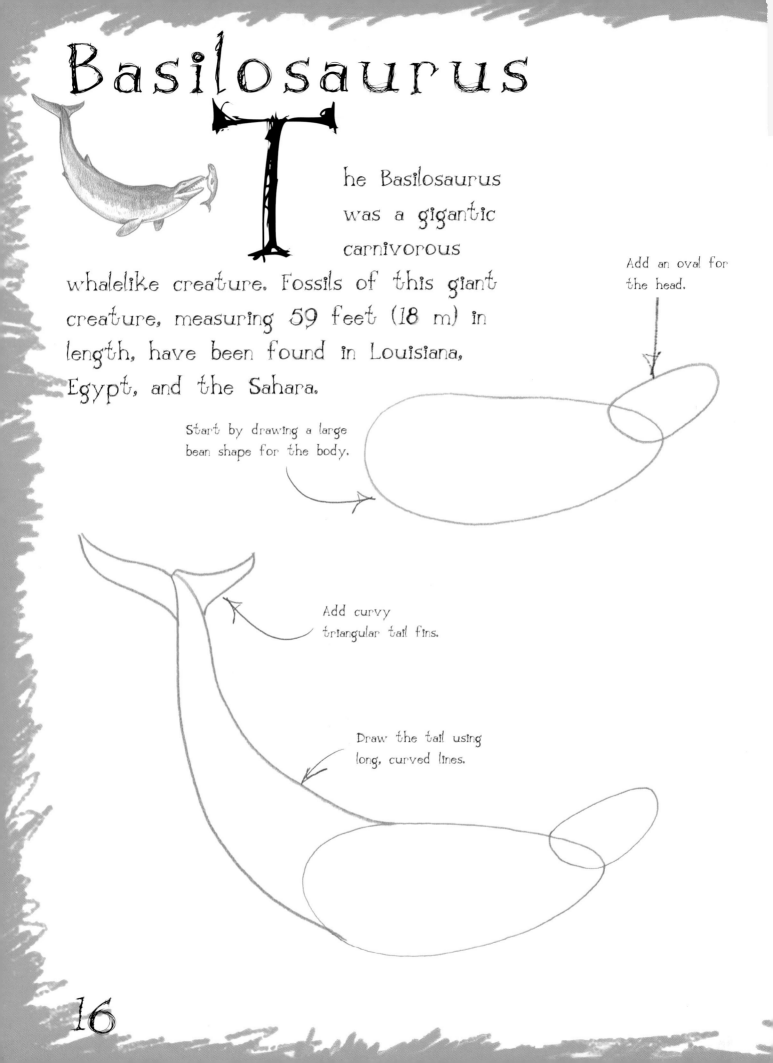

The Basilosaurus was a gigantic carnivorous whalelike creature. Fossils of this giant creature, measuring 59 feet (18 m) in length, have been found in Louisiana, Egypt, and the Sahara.

Add an oval for the head.

Start by drawing a large bean shape for the body.

Add curvy triangular tail fins.

Draw the tail using long, curved lines.

Add the eyes.

Sketch in the jagged sharp teeth.

Add small fins to the body.

Add two large flippers.

Using a Mirror
Try looking at your drawing in a mirror. Seeing it in reverse can help you spot mistakes.

Add tone to the back. Keep your pencil line in the same direction to create the skin effects.

Finish the detail of the head.

Leave white areas along the body to show the sheen of the skin.

Add some prey for the Basilosaurus.

Remove any unwanted construction lines.

Indricotherium

Indricotherium lived around 30 to 25 million years ago. This large land mammal would have eaten the tallest parts of trees in the same way a giraffe does.

Draw two large ovals for the body. Add a line at the top for the spine.

Draw the thick back legs.

Add a curved underbelly.

Draw the front legs, overlapping them to indicate that one leg is behind the other.

Add two long, curved lines for the thick neck.

Sketch in the eyes, nose, and ears.

Use curving lines to show the shape of the head.

Draw curved lines around the body to suggest muscle structure.

Draw small semicircles for the toes.

Add tone to define the shape of the head.

Add lots of lines to indicate the leathery skin folds of the body.

Add a long, curvy tail.

Add bristles at the end of the tail.

Shade in areas where light wouldn't reach.

Add in the ground.

Remove any unwanted construction lines.

19

Phorusrhacos

Phorusrhacos is known as one of the terror birds. It stood 10 feet (3 m) tall and fed on small mammals and carcasses.

Draw an oval for the head.

Draw a curved line for the neck.

Draw a larger oval for the body.

Add a second curved line for the neck.

Sketch in the basic shape of the tail.

Draw in the legs with long, curved lines.

Add construction lines to position the base of the feet.

Composition

By framing your drawing with a square or a rectangle, you can make it look completely different.

Sketch in the shape of the curving beak and position the eye.

Sketch in construction lines for the head plumage.

Using the construction lines as a guide, draw the feather shapes of the head plumage.

Add another line to the neck.

Add a jagged line for where the feathers overlap the leg.

Add tone to the beak and finish the head details.

Add lots of curved lines for the feathered plumage.

Shade areas where light wouldn't reach.

Add toes and talons to the feet.

Add lines to create skin texture.

Sketch tonal stripes onto the legs.

Add the ground.

Remove any unwanted construction lines.

21

Woolly Rhino

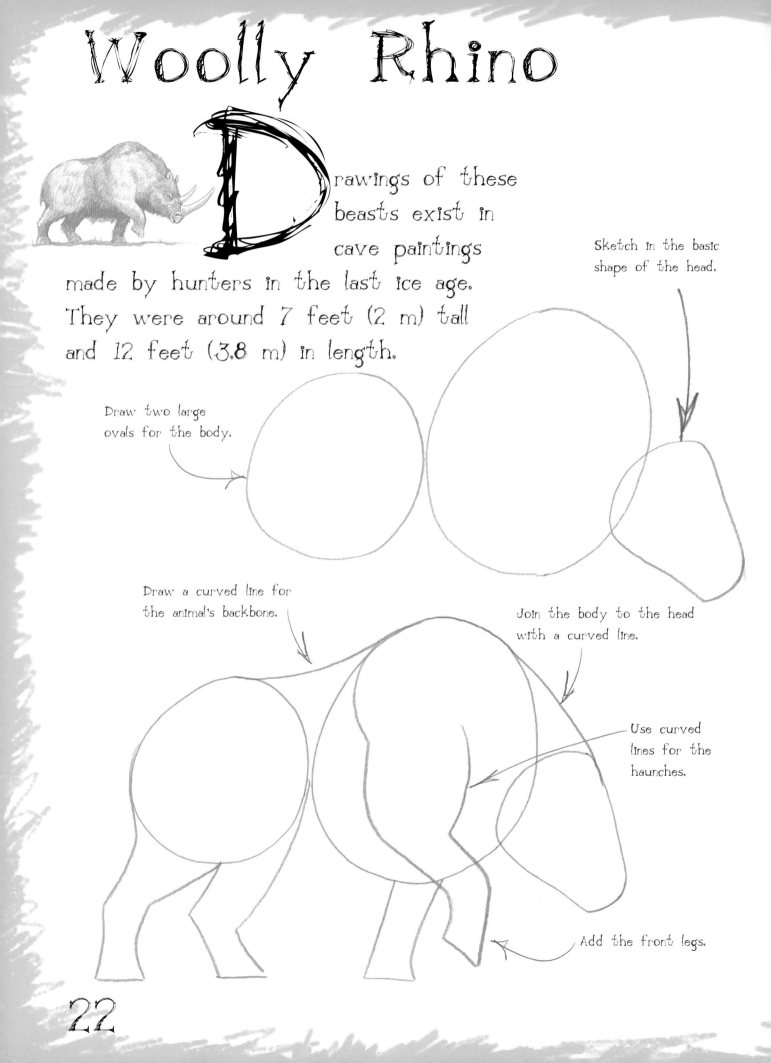

Drawings of these beasts exist in cave paintings made by hunters in the last ice age. They were around 7 feet (2 m) tall and 12 feet (3.8 m) in length.

Draw two large ovals for the body.

Sketch in the basic shape of the head.

Draw a curved line for the animal's backbone.

Join the body to the head with a curved line.

Use curved lines for the haunches.

Add the front legs.

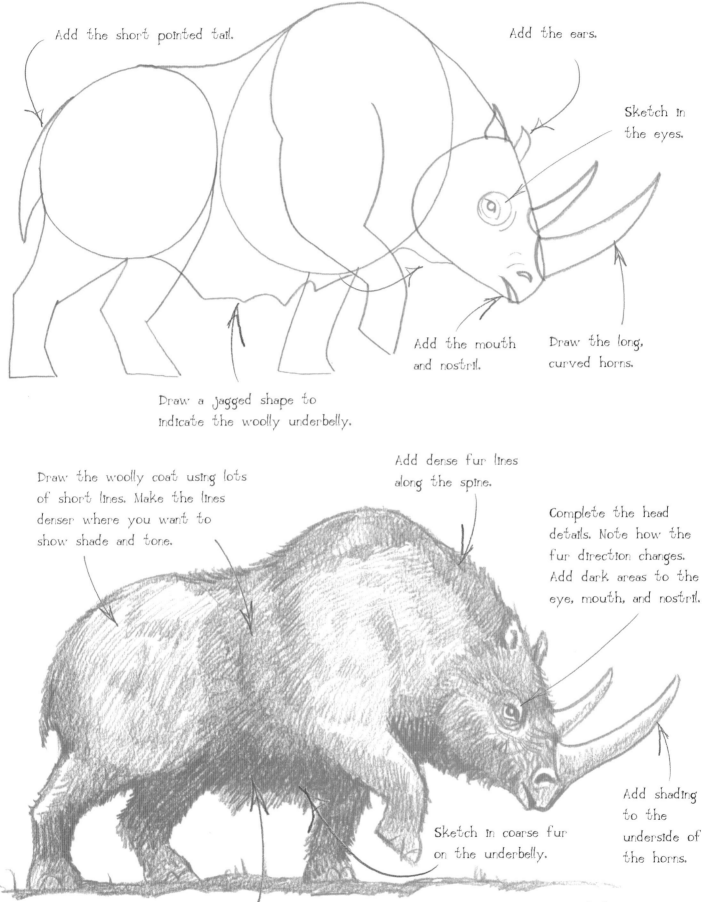

Add the short pointed tail.

Add the ears.

Sketch in the eyes.

Add the mouth and nostril.

Draw the long, curved horns.

Draw a jagged shape to indicate the woolly underbelly.

Draw the woolly coat using lots of short lines. Make the lines denser where you want to show shade and tone.

Add dense fur lines along the spine.

Complete the head details. Note how the fur direction changes. Add dark areas to the eye, mouth, and nostril.

Sketch in coarse fur on the underbelly.

Add shading to the underside of the horns.

Add the ground.

Add darker tone to areas light wouldn't reach.

Remove any unwanted construction lines.

23

Megatherium

This giant ground sloth stood 20 feet (6 m) high and weighed around 4 tons (3.8 t)! It lived 1.9 million to 80,000 years ago.

Chiaroscuro

Add dark shading to parts of your drawing for a dramatic effect.

Draw two large ovals for the body.

Add a curved line for the spine.

Sketch in the basic shape of the head.

Add a curved line for the neck.

Draw a long, curved line for the belly.

Use curved lines to draw the legs.

Add long, pointed toes.

Add the eye, nostril, ear, and downturned mouth.

Sketch a jagged line around the outline to indicate fur.

Sketch in the arms with long, pointed fingers.

Finish drawing the head details.

Draw the fur using lots of short lines. Vary the frequency for areas of light and dark.

Sketch in a curved tail.

Use many short lines to define the arms.

Draw a tree and shrubbery for added effect.

Add shading to where light won't reach.

Remove any unwanted construction lines.

25

Smilodon

This large sabre-tooth cat hunted grazing animals. It pinned them down with its powerful front legs and killed them with its bite. Males could reach 10 feet (3 m) in height.

Negative Space
Always check the negative space, or the area around your drawing. This can help you spot mistakes.

Start by drawing two ovals.

Join the two ovals with a curved line for the spine.

Add two curved lines for the neck to join the head to the body.

Sketch in the shape of the head.

Add a line for the belly.

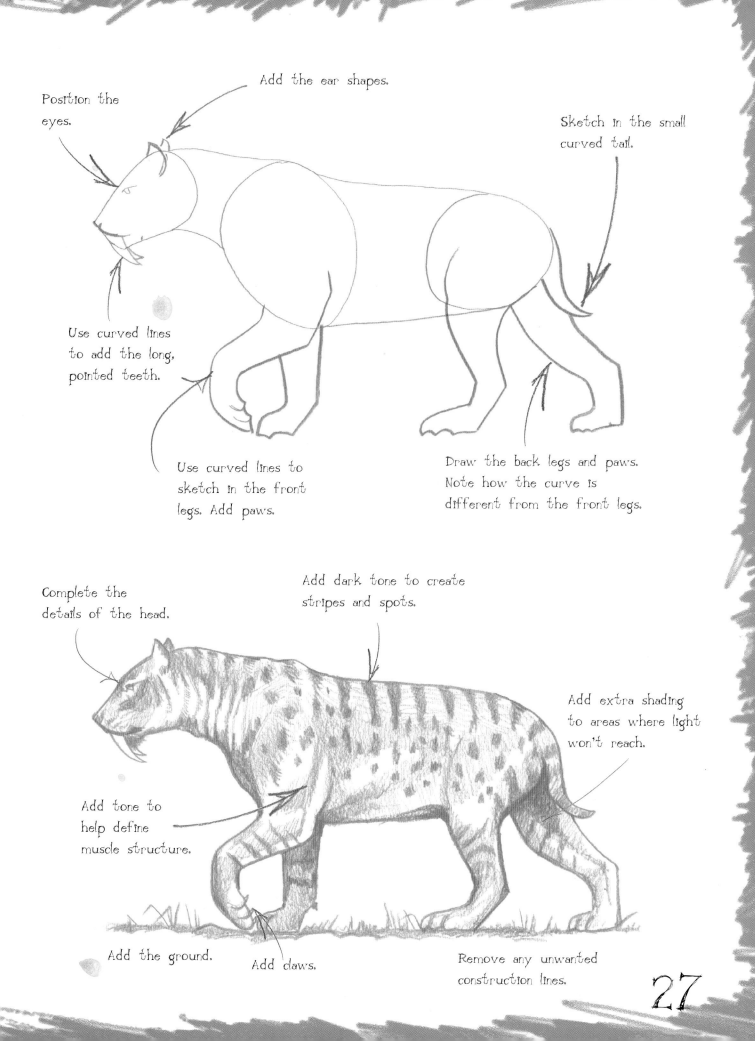

Position the eyes.

Add the ear shapes.

Sketch in the small curved tail.

Use curved lines to add the long, pointed teeth.

Use curved lines to sketch in the front legs. Add paws.

Draw the back legs and paws. Note how the curve is different from the front legs.

Complete the details of the head.

Add dark tone to create stripes and spots.

Add extra shading to areas where light won't reach.

Add tone to help define muscle structure.

Add the ground.

Add claws.

Remove any unwanted construction lines.

27

Woolly Mammoth

These giants of the ice age grazed on vegetation. Males could grow to a height of 10 feet (3 m). Bones and frozen carcasses have been found from Ireland to Siberia, in Russia, and many places throughout Europe.

Start by drawing three overlapping ovals.

Add curved lines to link the three ovals together.

Draw in long, curved lines to add the thick front legs.

Note how the back legs curve differently from the front legs.

Sketch in an eye and an ear.

Sketch long, curved lines for the trunk.

Add long, curved lines for the tusks.

Add a line for the tail.

Add a dark, coarse patch of hair on top of the mammoth's head.

Draw lots of short lines for the mammoth's fur. Vary the frequency to create areas of light and dark.

Darken the areas around the eye and ear.

Vary the fur length and make some areas more coarse and straggly.

Add dark tone to areas where light would not reach.

Add a line of tone to the tusks for a three-dimensional effect.

Add the ground.

Remove any unwanted construction lines.

29

Attack!

A Doedicurus is under attack by a Phorusrhacos. The well-armored Doedicurus can defend itself with its spiky tail.

Draw a large oval for the body of the Phorusrhacos.

Use straight lines to sketch in the position of the legs.

Draw two overlapping ovals for the body and head of the Doedicurus.

Sketch in an oval for the head and connect it to the body with a curved neck.

Add another line to each leg.

Draw the curved lines for the tail and add an oval at the end.

Draw the basic shape for the wings.

Sketch in the head plumage.

Add the eye and beak.

Position the eyes, ears, and mouth.

Draw the tail spikes.

Sketch in the tail shape.

Add armored bands to the tail.

Draw the three-toed claws.

Add the legs with three spiked toes.

Add areas of tone to define the body shapes.

Complete the details of the Phorusrhacos.

Draw many small ovals around the body to create the armored exterior.

Remove any unwanted construction lines.

Draw a background for added drama.

31

Glossary

chiaroscuro (kee–AHR–uh–skyur–oh) The practice of drawing high–contrast pictures with a lot of black and white but not much gray.

composition (kom–puh–ZIH–shun) The arrangement of the parts of a picture on the drawing paper.

construction lines (kun–STRUK–shun LYNZ) Guides used in the early stages of a drawing. They are erased later.

perspective (per–SPEK–tiv) A method of drawing in which near objects are shown larger than faraway objects to give an impression of depth.

proportion (pruh–POR–shun) The correct relationship of scale between each part of the drawing.

silhouette (sih–luh–WET) A drawing that shows only a flat dark shape, like a shadow.

sketchbook (SKECH–buk) A book in which sketches are made.

vanishing point (VA–nish–ing POYNT) The place in a perspective drawing where parallel lines appear to meet.

Index

Web Sites

Due to the changing nature of Internet links, PowerKids Press has developed an online list of Web sites related to the subject of this book. This site is updated regularly. Please use this link to access the list:

www.powerkidslinks.com/htd/mammoth/